Ashlin

Emellee

no

Deryk

219

The Usborne
Little Book
of
Cats and
Kittens

First published in 2009 by Usborne Publishing Ltd.,
Usborne House, 83-85 Saffron Hill, London, ECIN 8RT, England
www.usborne.com

The Usborne
Little Book
of
Cats and
Kittens

Sarah Khan

Designed by Kate Rimmer

Illustrated by Stephen Lambert

Digital manipulation by Keith Furnival

Consultant: Amanda Thomas

Edited by Kirsteen Rogers

Internet links

The Usborne Quicklinks Website is packed with thousands of links to all the
best websites on the internet. The websites include information, video
clips, sounds, games and animations that support and enhance
the information in Usborne internet-linked books.

To visit the recommended websites for the *Little Book of Cats and Kittens*, go
to the Usborne Quicklinks Website at **www.usborne-quicklinks.com**
and enter the keywords: **little cats**

Internet safety

When using the internet please follow the internet safety guidelines
displayed on the Usborne Quicklinks Website. The websites recommended
in Usborne Quicklinks are regularly reviewed. However, the content of a
website may change at any time and Usborne Publishing is not responsible
for the content of websites other than its own. We recommend that
children are supervised while on the internet.

Contents

About cats

This playful pet kitten belongs to the same family as ferocious lions, tigers and leopards.

All over the world, cats are loved and cherished as pets. The cats that people keep as pets are described as domesticated.

All in the family

Domesticated cats belong to the same family as wild, bigger cats such as lions and tigers. If you watch a pet cat play-hunting, you might see it behaving in the same way as its wilder relatives.

The taming of the cat

Many experts believe that Ancient Egyptians used to take cats hunting and fishing, and trained them to retrieve the animals they killed.

Cats have been living with people for over 2,000 years. The Ancient Egyptians tamed wild, desert-dwelling cats to act as rat-catchers and protect their grain stores from ravenous rodents.

What makes a cat a cat?

All cats are mammals, which means they grow hair, produce their own body heat, feed their babies with milk, and have different types of teeth for cutting and chewing food. Lots of animals, including people, have these abilities, but there are other clever things that only cats can do, such as purring, and landing on their feet after a fall. Also, no matter what the size or type, all cats share the same basic body shape and features.

From huge jungle tigers to little domestic cats like this one, all the members of the cat family have certain features in common.

Only cats can...

...land on their feet after falling from a height...

...purr when happy...

...and draw their claws into their paws.

Big eyes

Large, soft ears

Long, flexible spine

Whiskers on face

Flexible tail

Body types

Although all cats have the same basic body shape, there are subtle differences in their build and features. These differences have led cat experts to group cats into three main body types.

Shorthairs

Most cats you'll see have short, dense fur, so are described as shorthairs. Apart from their fur, they also have other characteristics in common.

Shorthairs tend to have curvy features – their ears, eyes, head, tail and paws are all arched or rounded. They also have stocky, powerful bodies and short, strong legs. This build is sometimes described as "cobby."

Cats with shorter coats need a lot less grooming than those with long hair.

This shorthair is from Britain. American and European shorthairs tend to be a little slimmer.

Longhairs

Some cats have long, silky fur, which gives them a pampered appearance. Called longhairs or Persians, these cats have varying lengths of fur on different parts of their bodies.

Longhairs tend to have smaller ears than other cats and also shorter, thicker legs.

You can see the extra-long fur around this longhair's ears and neck. It also has longer fur on its back legs and tail, and between its front legs. Elsewhere, its hair is shorter.

Most foreign cats have long ears and a wedge-shaped head.

Foreign cats

When dividing cats into body types, experts class Asian cats with long bodies and long legs as foreign cats. Most have short fur, but you may see some with longer coats. They are most easily recognized by their narrow faces and oval-shaped paws.

Shades and patterns

Every cat is unique. Even if two cats seem identical at first glance, a closer look will reveal that each one has its own distinct patterns and shades.

Coats of many colors

Cats' coats come in an amazing variety of shades, from black, white and brown, to more subtle hues of smoke, lilac and even blue. A cat can be just one shade, or the colors can combine to form patterns.

Bicolor pattern

Common patterns

Solid coats are the easiest to recognize because they are just one color all over.

Tabby pattern

Bicolor and **tricolor** coats are white with patches of one or two other colors. The patches can be solid or patterned.

Tabby cats' coats are covered with dark patterns of stripes, spots and swirls.

Pointed pattern

Pointed cats have faces, paws and tails that are darker than the rest of their bodies.

A kitten's pattern may change over time. This young spotted shorthair is striped now, but will become more spotted as it grows.

Cats that are speckled or shimmer when they move, may have hairs that are made up of bands of different colors.

Shaded parts

Some cats have a colored patch of fur, called a blaze, running down the forehead to the nose. At the end of the nose, a cat's skin is either pink or black and often matches the skin under its paws.

Also, if you look at the color of a cat's whiskers, you'll see that it matches one of the shades of its coat. Tortoiseshell cats, for example, (also called calico cats in the USA) are covered in patches of white, black and orange. Their whiskers can be white, black, or a mixture of both. Curiously, no cat ever has orange whiskers.

Tortoiseshell cats, like this one, can only have black or white-colored whiskers.

Spotted tabby shorthairs tend to be active, athletic cats.

Kinds of cats

Most cats are a mix of types, but cats of a specific breed have certain features in common. Worldwide, there are over 70 breeds of cats. Here are some common ones:

Tabby shorthairs have coats with dark striped, spotted or wavy markings and an M-shaped mark on their foreheads. They tend not to need much grooming or fussing over.

Abyssinians are originally from Ethiopia. They have short, speckled coats, and graceful, muscular bodies. Intelligent, curious cats, they enjoy exploring and need lots of attention.

Bicolor shorthairs have big, round heads, and are covered in patches of colors and white. They are intelligent cats that are easy to train.

No matter how closely you look, you'll never find any stray white hairs in the black parts of a black and white shorthair's coat.

Siamese cats are elegant animals with light-colored coats that darken to brown, blue or lilac around their tails, ears, faces and legs. They tend to want lots of attention and entertainment, which they ask for by meowing loudly.

This Siamese kitten's vivid blue, almond-shaped eyes are a feature common to all Siamese cats.

Colorpoints or **Himalayans** are like Siamese cats with longer fur and quieter voices. They are usually very playful and affectionate, and have silkier fur than other longhaired cats.

Blue longhairs are the most popular longhaired breed.

Blue longhair kittens can be born with tabby markings, but these disappear as they grow. The adults have blue-gray fur and flat faces. Like most longhair cats, they are generally quiet and gentle.

Burmese cats usually have wedge-shaped heads.

Burmese cats originally came from Thailand. They have muscular, compact bodies with short, glossy coats and yellow-gold eyes. Often playful, they are friendly toward people.

When this little Maine Coon kitten grows up, it'll have a heavy coat and a long, thick tail.

Unusual cats

Over the generations, breeds of cats with one or more strange or unusual features occasionally develop. These cats are usually very rare, especially outside the country where they first appeared.

Maine Coons get their name from the American state they originally came from, and their large size and shaggy coat which makes them look like raccoons.

Manx cat

Manx cats are an old breed from the Isle of Man – a small island off the west coast of England. Most are completely tailless, but others have little stumps instead of tails.

Scottish Fold

Scottish Folds are so named because of their nationality and their distinctive, folded-down ears. At birth, their ears are straight, but begin to fold down after around four weeks.

Somali cats are longhaired versions of Abyssinian cats (see page 12). Shy around people, their bushy tails and large, pricked ears make them look very similar to foxes.

Bombay cats look like little panthers. They have thick, shiny, solid black coats, large gold or copper-colored eyes, and they purr very loudly.

Sphynx cats look totally bald, but are actually covered with soft, almost invisible hairs. Their skin tends to be wrinkly.

Si-rex cats have big, piercing blue eyes, wide, wedge-shaped heads, and thin, crinkled coats and whiskers.

Japanese bobtails are an ancient breed with puffy, pom-pom tails. Each cat's tail is kinked or curved at a different angle, which means that no two Japanese bobtails' tails are ever exactly the same.

Nicknamed "pixie cats" and "alien cats," Si-rexes have massive eyes and ears. These features are particularly noticeable in Si-rex kittens, like these.

Having kittens

Unless you want to breed your cat, you should take it to the vet for an operation to stop it from having kittens.

Cats are independent creatures that don't need much help during pregnancy. But there are a few things you can do to make a mother cat's life as easy as possible.

Making a kitten box

- ☀ Find a quiet and sheltered place where your cat will feel comfortable.

- ☀ Cover the floor with newspaper and then place a cardboard box on top.

- ☀ Cut a section out of one side of the box. Line the box with newspaper.

- ☀ It's a good idea to put a blanket in the box, but it will need washing daily.

Staying out of harm's way

A pregnant cat can be carrying as many as eight hungry kittens, packed tightly inside and dependent on her for nourishment. But alongside a bellyful of kittens there's not much room for a bowlful of food, so a pregnant cat needs to eat little and often.

When she feels the time is close, she will start snooping around in closets or under beds for a safe place to give birth. She's looking for a spot that's snug and warm and out of the way of prying eyes and clumsy feet. To help her, you can make a kitten box (see left).

A kitten box should be a quiet haven for your cat, so try not to disturb her too much while she's resting there.

The big day

A cat's pregnancy lasts about nine weeks, but exactly when the kittens are due is always a mystery. You could well wake one morning to the sight of a tired mother, and a warm jumble of mewing kittens.

She'll lick each new arrival with her rough tongue, to start its breathing, before suckling the kittens with her milk for the first time.

After all your careful planning, your cat may still decide she prefers a different spot, such as the bottom of your closet.

This mother cat will suckle her kittens until they are about two months old and ready to move on to solid food.

From kitten to cat

Kittens grow from helpless infanthood to graceful adulthood before a human baby has even said its first word. But in old age the pace of a cat's life slows to a stately saunter.

A bundle of fur

A newborn kitten is so small that it can be cradled in the palm of a hand and weighs no more than a plum. Its eyes and ears are shut tight and it has to snuggle up to its brothers and sisters to keep warm.

After six days, these kittens will open their eyes for the first time.

Growing up fast

A mother cat feeds her kittens regularly with milk from her body. Kittens spend most of their time asleep so that the energy from the milk is not wasted in movement, and can be used instead to help their fragile bodies grow.

A mother cat's milk is full of calories and proteins, which help her kittens to grow quickly.

Within three weeks this kitten is already learning to use its young legs.

Pushing boundaries

Kittens are mischievous and filled with curiosity about the world around them. They're lively and playful, pouncing and bouncing around as they explore their new surroundings. But they also tire easily, and can fall asleep in the most unusual places.

By the time a kitten is one year old, it is fully grown and confident in its adulthood. Dapper and strong-willed, most cats enjoy a game, but won't be afraid to stroll away once they've had enough.

The comforts of old age

Cats begin to slow down as their bodies age. Enjoying the life of a senior citizen, they can often be found in their favorite snuggery, sleeping the day away in peace and quiet.

Kittens can fall asleep almost anywhere.

While grappling with their toys, kittens are honing their hunting skills.

As a cat ages, it will wander its neighborhood less and less, preferring to keep to its own yard.

If you choose a fluffy kitten,
like this one, there's a good
chance that it will have long
fur when it grows up.

Adopting a kitten

Having a cat of your own can be lots of fun,
but is a serious responsibility, too. Before
you get one, try to think about all the
pros and cons of having a pet, and to be as
prepared as you can for your new arrival.

What to look for

If you choose an adult cat, you will be
able to get an idea of its personality.
A kitten's personality may be harder
to judge, but it will settle into a
new home more quickly than an
older cat.

To find a pet, you can ask your
friends if they know anyone whose
cats have recently had kittens. Vets
and animal shelters might also have
cats who are in need of a home.

If you are getting a kitten from
a friend, you could ask to see its
mother and inquire about her health
and personality, because your kitten
might develop the same features as
its parent.

To choose a kitten that looks clean and healthy, look for these signs:

Healthy coat

Clean and dry under tail

Clean ears

Bright eyes

Clean nose

If you can, gently look inside the kitten's mouth to check that it has a full set of teeth.

Sturdy legs

Strong paws

Pets with personality

Every kitten has its own personality. If you watch one at play, you might pick up some clues as to what it is like. Choose one that's lively, but not aggressive.

Whether bold or timid, your kitten will soon start investigating its new surroundings when you bring it home. Before it has a chance to explore, pick up the things from the floor of the house that might be dangerous, such as wires, and small objects that a kitten could swallow.

Strong, active kittens will probably need to be played with often.

A timid kitten can take longer to adapt to a new home.

Caring for a kitten

A kitten is usually ready to leave its mother when it's between two and three months old. When you bring your kitten home, there are lots of things you can do to help it get comfortable in its new surroundings.

Settling in

It's a good idea to have all the things your kitten needs ready to use as soon as it arrives. That way, you can begin taking care of your pet right away, and it can start getting used to all its new accessories. Make sure that the things it will be using for a long time, such as its bed, food bowls and litter tray, are easy to clean.

Here are the things you need to take care of your kitten...

- Some cans or packages of kitten food

- Separate dishes for food and water

- A plastic litter tray, half-filled with cat litter

- A warm, comfortable bed

- A scratching post for claw-sharpening

- A few different types of cat toys

- A cat brush

You can make your cat a bed using a shallow, sturdy cardboard box.

Kittens will get to know their new things by touching, sniffing and playing with them.

It might take a while for your kitten to get used to its new environment. While it explores your home, follow quietly. To make a new place seem less strange, cats rub themselves against things so their own scent mixes with the smells of the unfamiliar objects.

As this kitten explores its new home, it's best not to pick it up at first, but let it wander undisturbed.

Pleased to meet you

To introduce yourself to your kitten, get its attention by crouching down and calling its name. Try holding out your hand – it might sniff your fingers to become used to your smell. After a while, you can pick the kitten up, but always use both hands.

If your new kitten starts crying for its mother, you can comfort it by holding and stroking it.

This kittens is very timid, so is approaching its new owner slowly and nervously.

Food and feeding

What and how often a cat eats plays a vital role in its development from a tiny, weak kitten into a strong, healthy adult.

Starting on solids

For about the first two months of their lives, kittens feed on their mother's milk, but most start to nibble at solid food before they're ready to move away to another home.

At around six months old, kittens lose their baby teeth and grow adult ones. They use long, sharp front teeth to tear solid food, and smaller side teeth to chew it.

Kittens' menu

* Specially formulated kitten food, dry or moist. It provides all the energy kittens need to grow.

Cats' menu

* Moist cat food is easier for older cats to chew.

* Dry cat food keeps a cat's teeth clean.

* Cat treats contain fiber, which keeps a cat's coat, skin and teeth healthy.

A month-old kitten starts to learn how to eat solid food by copying its mother.

Feeding time

Cats are creatures of habit – they like to be fed at the same times in the same place every day. To stop young kittens from eating too much or from getting too hungry in between feeds, it's best to give them four or five small meals of kitten food a day.

Cats don't like to be disturbed while they eat, so it's a good idea to keep their feeding bowl in a quiet corner.

When a kitten is about six months old, you can start cutting down its meal times to two or three a day, but give it bigger portions. At around 12 months, you can start feeding it adult cat food.

Cats will ignore their water bowl or, like this kitten, just play with it if the water isn't fresh.

Whatever your cat's age, it always needs a supply of fresh drinking water. Cats that eat mainly dry food drink more often.

Even if a cat's upper layer of fur is wet, its skin stays warm and dry.

Fur care

A cat's fur is more than just a pretty layer of fluff – it's a vital protective covering. Most cats have at least two layers of fur: the upper layer is a little oily to keep water from soaking through, and the under layer is made up of fluffy hairs that keep the cat warm.

Licking clean

Cats lick their fur to keep it clean and comb out knots. As a cat licks itself, it leaves tiny, dried flakes of saliva in its fur, which can cause allergic reactions, such as itching and sneezing, in some people.

Cats swallow some loose fur as they lick themselves. Inside the cat's body, the hair clogs together into balls that the cat coughs up from time to time.

For a mother cat, like this one, licking is not only the best method of grooming her kitten, but also a good way to bond with it.

Out with the old

When hairs on a cat's coat are damaged or old, they fall away. Cats lose hair all the time, but shed most heavily in spring. During winter, their fur grows thicker to keep them warm but, when spring comes, they don't need the extra fur anymore. Spring shedding is particularly noticeable in cats who spend lots of time outside, because their winter coats grow thicker than those of indoor cats.

Cats that stay indoors most of the time shed less hair than those that are allowed outside.

How to brush a cat

You can help your cat to get rid of loose fur by brushing its coat regularly. Shorthairs only need this doing about once a week, but longhairs need more frequent brushing. If you start this routine when you first get your cat, it will become used to being brushed and might come to enjoy it.

Always be gentle when brushing your cat.

Brushing a cat

1. Before you start, stroke your cat to relax it and help it get used to being handled.

2. Lay an old blanket or towel on your lap or on a table and sit your cat on top.

3. Brush the fur in the direction that it grows, starting with the cat's back, then moving on to the legs and tail.

4. Brush under its chin and around its ears. Avoid its eyes, and only brush its stomach if it likes it.

Training a kitten...

Kittens aren't as easy to train as puppies, but it's a good idea to try to teach your new pet what it can and can't do in your home.

Once it has learned its name, your kitten might come when you call it, with its tail up as a greeting, like this.

...to recognize its name

When you first get your cat, use its name as much as possible when playing with it, stroking it and calling it for a meal.

...to behave

If you see your kitten doing something it shouldn't, say its name and "No!" in a firm voice, then move it away.

...to use a cat flap

If you have a cat flap, you can train your kitten to use it at around four months old. Try tempting it from the other side of the door with a treat or toy. Keep the flap open the first few times, then close it and call its name.

You can reward good behavior with a treat, such as a teaspoon of yogurt or a small piece of cheese. Leftovers and chocolate might make your cat sick.

...to use a scratching post

Your cat will sharpen its claws on your furniture unless you train it to use a scratching post. Take it to the post and gently stretch out its front paws. Then, move its paws up and down the post.

...to use a litter tray

To teach your kitten to use its litter tray, try sitting it in the tray after it has finished eating, or when it's crouching down with its tail up, as this is a sign that it needs to go.

Put the scratching post near where your pet sleeps or naps, as cats like to scratch right after waking up.

Cat litter can come in a variety of forms, such as absorbent wooden pellets, like the ones in this tray, or smaller clay granules which clump together when wet.

Write your number on your cat's collar so that, if the cat wanders away, whoever finds it can call you.

Out and about

Indoor cats are generally safer and healthier than cats who are allowed outside. but many cats enjoy visiting the outdoors.

Stepping out

There are lots of alternatives for cats to be able to enjoy the outdoors without roaming free. You could buy or make your cat a window ledge or perch so that it can see outside. allow access to a screened-in patio or try a leash and cat harness for short walks. Other ideas include a variety of outdoor cat enclosures that you can buy or make.

If you decide to allow your cat outside, or to another room where a litter box is located, for example, a cat flap, like this one, is handy.

Going for a ride

If you're traveling with your cat in a car, bus or plane, the most convenient and comfortable way to carry it is in a sturdy pet carrier.

If you need to travel by plane with your cat, check with your airline for any specific requirements for pet carriers.

Getting used to its carrier, this kitten has been playing in it for a few days before it's due to travel.

When you go on vacation, it's best to get someone to feed your cat at home. If this isn't possible, you can board it at a pet hotel or in a boarding kennel at your vet's office. You can leave its blanket with it and some of its toys too, so it feels more at home.

Before you go away, it's important to check your cat's ID collar and license to ensure the information is up-to-date If you want, you could also look into other modern ID methods, such as microchipping or GPS locators.

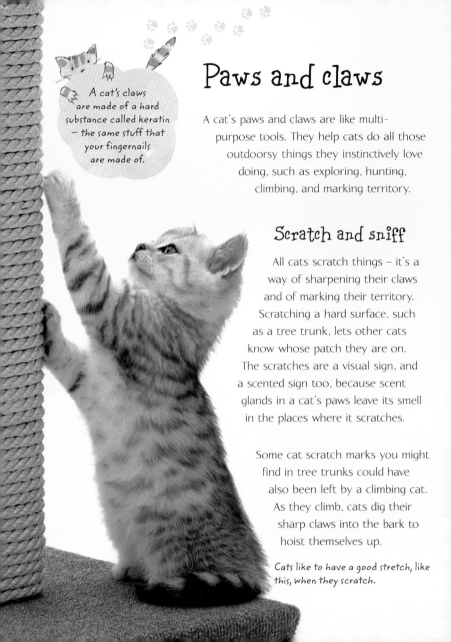

Paws and claws

A cat's paws and claws are like multi-purpose tools. They help cats do all those outdoorsy things they instinctively love doing, such as exploring, hunting, climbing, and marking territory.

A cat's claws are made of a hard substance called keratin – the same stuff that your fingernails are made of.

Scratch and sniff

All cats scratch things – it's a way of sharpening their claws and of marking their territory. Scratching a hard surface, such as a tree trunk, lets other cats know whose patch they are on. The scratches are a visual sign, and a scented sign too, because scent glands in a cat's paws leave its smell in the places where it scratches.

Some cat scratch marks you might find in tree trunks could have also been left by a climbing cat. As they climb, cats dig their sharp claws into the bark to hoist themselves up.

Cats like to have a good stretch, like this, when they scratch.

Paw pads

The squishy, cushioned parts on the underside of a cat's paws are called pads. They are very sensitive to changes in temperature and texture. Cats use their pads to investigate new and unfamiliar objects.

The skin covering a paw pad is rough and thick, protecting the foot and giving a firm grip on slippery surfaces.

While this kitten decides what to do with the strange thing it has just found, it touches the mystery object with the pads on its paws.

Silent steps

Most of the time, a cat's claws aren't on display, but are drawn into its paws. When stalking, the claws are tucked away, so they don't tap on the ground, letting the cat sneak up silently on its unsuspecting victim. The sound of a cat's footfalls are muffled even further by its cushioned pads and by fur between its toes.

Cats draw in their claws when they walk on hard surfaces, so the claws don't wear away too quickly.

Super senses

A cat's world is a patchwork of vivid sensations because, in the wild, its senses need to be sharp enough to pick up on any sign of its prey.

Picking up the scent

As it sets off on a hunt, a cat is alert for the smell of mouse: a quick sniff of the ground and it knows everything that's recently passed nearby.

Once it knows there's prey in the area, a cat tenses, and listens closely. The calls of mice and other small rodents are pitched too high for a human, but not for a cat; and its ears can swivel around to pinpoint the location of any careless squeak.

When a cat rubs against your leg, it is marking you with its scent, to let other cats know who you belong to.

When hunting, cats crouch low like this to stop their silhouette from standing out against the night sky.

34

Night vision

At night and on the prowl, cats call upon another keen sense: their eyesight. The faint glow of the stars, or a sliver of moon, is all they need to spot an unsuspecting mouse in the undergrowth.

The golden-green gleam of a cat's eyes at night is light being reflected by a "mirror" at the back of each eye.

Whisker navigation

While cats have wonderful night vision, they have trouble seeing things up close. To avoid hurting themselves, they use their whiskers, which are so sensitive they can detect an obstacle simply by the way air currents swirl around it. Without them, a cat would bustle into leaves and branches while trying to sneak up on its prey.

This kitten is learning that its whiskers will help it to avoid poking its nose where it shouldn't.

Fussy eaters

Cats are natural-born hunters, and usually dislike any food other than meat and fish. They might ignore fruit and plants, because these get much of their flavor from sugar, which is a taste that passes unnoticed through most feline mouths.

Tuna, salmon, or chunks of beef, chicken or turkey make a tasty treat for your cat.

As this cat speeds along, it bends and stretches its body to take long strides and uses its back legs to push itself forward.

Cats on the move

Packed into a cat's little body are 290 bones and 517 muscles. Having so many joints and muscles makes a cat very flexible and agile, helping it to run, jump and even fall.

On the run

Going full speed, cats can run at about 45kph (30mph), which is as fast as a moped. They can only run at this speed for about a minute, though. After that, they have to stop and pant to cool down.

If this cat moves its head in one direction it will move its tail the opposite way to stop it from falling off the fence.

Balancing act

When walking, a cat places one paw in front of the other, as if it were treading a line. This helps it to walk along narrow ledges and fences. To keep it balanced, it uses its tail, a little like tightrope walkers who use long poles.

Jumping up...

For their size, cats can jump much higher and further than people can. They have muscly hind legs and strong hind paws that they use to push themselves off the ground.

As this cat jumps, it can reach up over seven times its own height.

...and down

There is an old superstition that cats have nine lives. This may come from a cat's ability to jump down from high places without breaking any bones or falling over on impact, and even to survive accidental falls from greater heights with few, if any, injuries.

Cats don't have collarbones, and their backbones are very flexible. This lets them bend and rotate their bodies to land feet first. If a cat falls even a short distance, it can almost always twist itself round as it drops, to land on its feet.

As a cat falls, it first turns its head and front legs, then the rest of its body follows.

With its body stretched out and front legs extended, this cat is in a perfect position for a safe landing.

37

Hunting

Even the most well-fed, domesticated cats love to hunt. The thrill and skill of hunting keeps them fit and adds a little excitement to their lives.

Silent but deadly

Cats can keep still for hours, watching quietly for prey. When a cat spots a possible victim, it begins to stalk. Crouching low with its head, body and tail held about level and its ears pricked, it glides silently forward.

Getting close to its prey, a cat freezes low, raises its bottom and begins to swing it from side to side with the tip of its tail twitching with excitement. Finally, the cat pounces on its victim.

Sometimes, when a cat sees its prey, its teeth start to chatter. This is because it's imagining that it is biting the animal.

Cats sneak up on their prey, getting ready for a final dash and spring.

This playing kitten has pounced on its toy mouse, pinning it down with its front paws.

Cats aren't fussy when it comes to hunting: they'll try to catch any small animal, from a beetle to a baby rabbit. Usually, pet cats don't eat their victims, but play with them for a while, either before or after killing them.

Playing with its toy prey is letting this kitten keep the thrill of the hunt going for as long as it can.

Giving a gift

Once a cat has caught its prey, it might give it to its owner as a present. If your cat drops a lifeless little body at your feet, you might not be pleased, but this is actually the cat's way of showing affection.

As a cat pounces, the sudden jangle of its bell collar can frighten off its intended victims.

Saved by the bell

To protect the local wildlife, you can fit your cat with a bell collar. As the cat moves, the tinkling bell will scare away any potential prey nearby. Don't expect your cat to be too happy about this, though.

To a cat, eye contact is impolite, confrontational and threatening, so it will avoid anyone looking directly at it.

Cat communication

Like people, cats use language, combining sounds and body movements to communicate, both with their owners and with each other.

Cats who are familiar and friendly rub up against each other to exchange their scents.

Friendly cats

If a cat is pleased to see you, it will put its tail straight up and point its ears forward. It might also arch its back and make a chirruping noise to say "hello."

Happy cats

Purring is usually a sign that a cat is relaxed and content. When it's feeling completely at ease, your cat might roll over and show you its stomach.

A cat's stomach is sensitive, so a cat will only roll over like this for people it trusts.

Irritable cats

When a cat is annoyed, it swishes its tail from side to side and points its ears back. As it gets angrier, it will hiss or spit, fluff up its fur to make it look bigger, and put its claws out, ready to fight. A cat in this mood is best left well alone.

Scaredy cats

If cornered by an enemy, such as another cat or an aggressive dog, a cat can become frightened and back off as far as possible with its ears flattened back as a sign of fear. Searching for an escape route, its eyes might dart around, and it could also raise a warning paw to show its claws, ready to strike if its enemy comes any closer.

Chatty cats

Cats mainly use body language to communicate with each other but, when it comes to talking to their owners, many cats realize that they have to use their vocal skills too. Each cat uses its own variations of "meow", differing in pitch, rhythm and volume, depending on what it wants from its owner.

Cats only use meowing sounds when they want to communicate with a human, and won't meow at any other animal.

Spoiling for a fight, this cat is fluffing up its fur to look as big and scary as it can.

When frightened, cats back away, and try to make themselves as small as possible.

Siamese cats tend to meow when yawning, drawing attention to their boredom.

Keeping clean

Cleanliness is of utmost importance to cats. They wash their own fur regularly, but need help to keep their teeth and their accessories clean, too.

Coat cleaning

When cats use their mouths to clean their coats, they don't just wet their fur but also comb it out with their tongues and pull out any knots or dirt with their teeth. A cat can get into extraordinary positions to reach all the different parts of its body, bending itself almost double and sticking its legs up over its shoulders as it washes itself.

A cat stretches itself out to clean the side of its body.

As this kitten licks itself clean, little bristles on its tongue sweep away the dirt and comb out loose hairs.

Face-wipes

To wash its face
and ears, a cat
uses its paws like
a washcloth. It licks
the paws to make
them damp, then wipes
them around its ears, over
its head and down its face.

This cat will repeat its
face-washing routine
over and over
until it is
completely
clean.

Teeth brushing

Cats need to clean their teeth regularly,
just like people do. In the wild, tearing
through the skin and bone of their prey
brushes away germs from their teeth.

Pet cats need their owners to clean their
teeth for them, using special toothbrushes
and pastes or dental treats – dry treats that
"brush" the teeth while the cat chews them.

Most cats hate
the taste of mint, so
cat toothpaste comes
in flavors that they
like, such as fish
or chicken.

Hygiene routine

Because cats like to be clean, they like the
things they use to be clean, too. Food bowls
need washing daily and the litter in litter
trays needs changing often as well. The trays
themselves should be washed once a week.

Cats cover their droppings
so, even if a tray looks
unused, the litter may
still need changing.

Playtime

Cats of all ages love to play. Romping around keeps cats exercised and entertained, and also lets them practice their hunting skills.

Action and adventure

Kittens start playing with their mothers, brothers and sisters at an early age. Young kittens wrestle with and pounce on each other, and chase their mother's tail.

If a mother cat thinks her kittens' play has become too rough, she steps in, growling and swatting at them as a warning to calm down.

These playing kittens may look like they're fighting, but they are continually giving each other signals to say that this is just a game.

You might find your kitten hiding in the most unlikely places.

Even when a cat is on its own, its curiosity and love of exploring can still make for inventive playtimes. Cats can squeeze into the tightest of spaces and scramble onto the highest of ledges, just for the fun of it.

Climbing is a natural instinct for cats, and even young kittens might try to test out their skills on high surfaces. Getting down from these precarious positions may not be as easy, so it's a good idea to keep an eye on a climbing kitten, in case it needs rescuing.

Playing at hunting, this kitten is getting ready to pounce on its striped prey from a height.

The thrill of the chase

Cats love chasing and pouncing on toys, especially ones that roll around the floor or dangle on string. While it's playing with string, make sure your cat doesn't start eating it, or the chewed bits might build up inside its body and cause health problems.

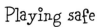

From time to time, let your cat catch the toy it has been chasing, otherwise it will become bored or annoyed.

Playing safe

Cats can get so carried away in a game, they harm themselves or whoever they're playing with. If a cat grabs you with its claws during play, calm it down by talking to it quietly, and slowly move it away from you. Then, walk away, so it knows it has done something you don't like.

It's best not to let your cat play with small things that it could swallow, such as marbles, or sharp things, such as scissors.

Kittens love the crunchy sound they make by chewing on a straw.

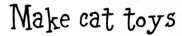

Make cat toys

Keeping your cat entertained doesn't have to cost a fortune in flashy new toys. You can make your own cat toys from items you might have just lying around at home.

Fill a wide-necked plastic bottle with treats, so the food can spill out easily.

On a roll

Rolling toys that can be chased are good for keeping cats busy when they're alone. You can use ping pong balls, scrunched-up paper balls, clean rolled-up socks, straws, or a cut-up cardboard tube. For a more rewarding toy, try putting some dry cat food inside an empty plastic water bottle. Leave the cap off and, as the cat rolls the bottle around, its food will come out bit by bit.

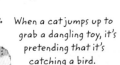
When a cat jumps up to grab a dangling toy, it's pretending that it's catching a bird.

Hanging around

A fun way to coax your cat to play with you is to dangle a stringed toy above its head. The toy can be any tough object that is large enough not to be swallowed, such as a pine cone, a baby's soft toy or an empty spool of thread. Whatever you choose, make sure that it's tied on tightly, so it doesn't come off too easily during play.

Boxes and bags

By putting out cardboard boxes and paper bags of different sizes, you can make a play area for your cat. Hiding treats and toys inside some of the containers adds an element of surprise. Never give a cat a plastic bag to play with though, as your pet might suffocate.

Kittens need to be supervized while they play, so making a play area like this is a good idea if you have more than one kitten to keep an eye on.

You can make this simple kitten playhouse by cutting holes out of a sturdy cardboard box.

Scrunched-up paper ball

Thread spool

Stuffed toy fish

Cat napping

After a strenuous play session or a hearty meal, there's nothing a cat likes to do more than settle down for a snooze. Cats are naturally active at night so can sleep for up to 16 hours during the day.

If a cat is dreaming, its eyes might move behind its eyelids, its legs might twitch, and its whiskers move around.

Deep sleep only comes to cats when they feel completely safe. You'll know a cat is sleeping soundly when it curls itself around into a ball.

Daylight dozing

Rather than having one long sleep, cats tend to rest in short naps. As it dozes, a cat's senses are still active and ready to spring into action. If it hears a noise or senses that someone is approaching, it will open its eyes to assess the situation before falling back asleep.

Even when napping, this cat's ears still twist around to pick up any sounds nearby.

Sleeping spots

When it comes to finding a place to sleep, cats can make some unusual choices. Even if it has its own bed, a cat might decide to have a nap somewhere else entirely, as long as it's comfortable and safe. When the weather is warm, it will search for a shaded place where it can stretch out. During cold periods, it will find somewhere warm to curl up.

This woolen hat makes a snug sleeping bag for a cold and tired kitten.

A long stretch

Upon waking after a long, deep sleep, a cat's body feels stiff and tight. It will have a good stretch to loosen its joints and get its body ready for the demands of the day.

Cats go through an elaborate routine of stretching movements. They lengthen out their backs, front legs and forelegs to get their blood flowing and prepare them for action.

Upon waking, cats first arch their back...

...then stretch out their front legs...

...then raise and stretch their back legs.

49

After dark

A cat in the wild sleeps during the day and hunts at night, when small animals scurry out of their burrows and nests looking for food. This is a cat's natural behavior, and as your domestic cat is really just a tame wild cat, its instincts are the same.

Wide awake and stalking around a sleeping household, your cat may get bored and demand attention.

Night terrors

Homes can become hunting grounds if a cat is not very active during the day. As it prowls the rooms, mice under the floorboards or cats outside can frustrate a confined cat and provoke a fit of yowling loud enough to wake the house.

Flooring and furniture may be scratched and attacked.

Fortunately, there are ways to avoid sleepless nights and a grouchy cat. The simplest solution is to make sure your cat gets plenty of active play during the day.

It's best not to let your cat play on your bed during the day as, at night, it might want to continue using your bed as its playground.

If your cats goes outside during the day, make sure it comes in at night.

Sleep soundly

If you want your cat to follow your own sleeping pattern you need to tire it out during the day. This will take plenty of dedication, but can form a close bond between you and your cat.

Set aside an hour in the evening so the two of you can play together with a favorite toy. Crouching and pouncing in play, your cat exhausts its desire to hunt. A few mouthfuls of food to round off the chase, and your contented cat can snuggle down to sleep.

It can take several weeks for a cat to get used to its new routine and change its sleeping pattern.

Playing with your cat in the evening can save your good night's sleep.

These kittens are tired out after a hard day's mischief-making.

Cat-friendly places

Many cats particularly like to chew a type of grass called cocksfoot. It has long, broad leaves, so is easy for them to bite.

If your cat visits outside make sure it stays in your yard. Cats like to roam and, if your cat digs in gardens, chews grass, kills wildlife or uses the bathroom in yards, it could annoy your neighbors. Many states also have leash laws to consider.

An area of fine soil that is enclosed by bushes and easily accessible from the house is a good spot for a cat's bathroom.

A place to go

If your cat goes outside, make sure you provide an area for it to use as a bathroom. You can spread some cat litter over an area of soil somewhere private and secluded, as cats don't like to use the bathroom with an audience watching. If you have a cat enclosure, you can put a small litter tray inside it.

Some experts think that eating grass helps cats to vomit, getting rid of any fur they might have swallowed.

Poisonous plants

As long as there are no pesticides or fertilizers, it's fine if your cat eats grass. But chewing other plants might be harmful, as some are poisonous to cats. To put them off, you can surround plants with things that cats hate the smell and feel of, such as citrus peel, stone chippings or pieces of eggshell.

Here are some common plants that are poisonous to cats...

- 🐾 Foxglove
- 🐾 Geranium
- 🐾 Lily
- 🐾 Marigold
- 🐾 Narcissus
- 🐾 Rhododendron

Crazy for catnip

The smell of a type of herb called catnip or catmint makes most cats very playful, sending them scampering or rolling around in delight. You can grow catnip in your cat-friendly garden, as it's safe for cats to eat and thrives in any type of soil.

If you don't have a garden, you can grow catnip in pots indoors.

Staying healthy

For a cat to lead a healthy, happy life, it needs care and attention from its owner and regular trips to the vet for check-ups. It's a good idea to get a cat checked by a vet at least once a year.

Uninvited guests

Even the healthiest of cats can become infested by little animals, such as fleas, mites or worms, which live in their bodies or on their skin. To keep these from irritating your pet, give it regular doses of pest-control medicine, starting when it is an older kitten. The medicines come in a variety of forms, from drops and syrups to pills and sprays.

Here are some signs to look out for that may mean your cat is unwell:

- Not eating
- Eating too much
- Constant coughing
- Persistent sneezing
- Continual scratching

If, like this kitten, your cat scratches a lot in its ears and also has black, sooty deposits in there, it could have ear mites.

Vet visit calendar

At nine weeks old

A kitten needs to go to the vet for some vaccinations. These protect it from some serious illnesses, like cat flu and leukemia.

At three months old

A kitten needs a second dose of vaccinations.

Between four and six months old

If you don't want your cat to father or give birth to kittens, the vet can neuter or spay it with a simple operation.

Every year

A cat should be given booster injections to make sure it is always protected from diseases.

Growing old

Elderly cats can be too tired and frail to take care of themselves. They need their owners to brush them daily, trim their nails when necessary, and keep them agile by playing with them gently.

Some cat experts think that the vibrations produced when a cat purrs can heal it if it has broken bones.

After having its second round of shots, this three-month-old kitten should be kept indoors for two weeks.

As cats age, they become more prone to illness or injury and recover more slowly.

Cat shows

All over the world, thousands of cat-lovers regularly flock to shows where the healthiest, happiest and prettiest cats are assessed, and a lucky few judged to be the best of their kind.

Top cats

A cat show is made up of a number of separate, individual competitions. There can be different competitions for neutered cats, un-neutered cats, young kittens under ten months old, and older cats over seven years of age. Most of the competitions are only for pedigrees – cats whose ancestors have been of the same breed for at least three generations – but there are usually also competitions for non-pedigree household pets.

Some cat shows include agility competitions in which cats complete an obstacle course.

Each winner is awarded a ribbon stating which category it has won. There are usually different colored ribbons for first, second and third place.

The full package

A cat is judged on different aspects of its appearance and personality, depending on its breed and the category it is being shown in.

A pedigree cat is assessed by the standards for its breed, set by the association that holds the show. In household cats, judges look for good health, beauty and poise. In all categories, judges like to see cats that are relaxed and confident around people.

Long bushy tail

A cat show judge would look for these features on a pedigree blue point birman's body.

Ears spaced well apart

Round head

Silky coat

White paws

Getting involved

If you want to enter your cat into a competition, it's best to go along to a few shows first, to see what happens and talk to some of the participants. To find out how to take part, try looking on the organizer's website or writing in for an application form.

At a cat show, you could look at the types of accessories the owners have with them, such as blankets and grooming equipment, so you'll know what to bring when you take part.

How to draw cats

If you like cats, you might enjoy drawing them. Their variety of shades and patterns and range of facial expressions makes them the perfect subject for any budding artist. This water color and marker technique is a fun and simple way to capture a cat's unique personality.

1. Using water color paints, mix a watery orange color. Paint an oval body.

2. Mix a brighter shade of orange for some stripes. Paint them while the paper is still a little damp.

Fine marker line

3. When the paint is dry, draw an outline near the edge. Add lines for legs, and oval paws with claws.

4. Draw a face, whiskers and a tail. Draw quickly — it adds character if the drawing is a little lopsided.

Small cat

By changing the size, shape and the faces of the cats, you can give them different characters.

This cross cat has bristly fur and slanted lines above its eyes.

Long thin cat

Give a fat cat a small high face.

A scared cat, with circles with dots in them for eyes

Sleeping cats

Although active cats are brimming with character, there's no getting around the fact that they spend most of their lives snoozing, so it's useful to know how to draw a sleeping cat. You can easily adapt the technique shown on the opposite page to draw a cat curled up, fast asleep.

You can draw these cats on cardboard or paper to make your own cat-lovers' greeting cards, notepaper, gift wrap, gift tags... the possibilities are endless.

Lines for ears

1. Paint the oval water color blob on its side. Then, add the brighter stripes on the top.

2. Draw an outline. Add ears, a curved line for a back leg and three paws and claws at the bottom.

3. Draw face details, with two curved lines for eyes. Add a tail hanging down or curving around.

You can paint different colors and patterns for different types of cats.

For howling cats, draw open mouths and closed eyes high on their heads.

This cat has two kittens.

Myths and legends

Throughout history, the cool confidence and unhurried grace of cats has bred suspicion. Dogs are often so eager to please, and horses and cattle are so shy: why then are cats so rarely ruffled? What do they know that you don't? Perhaps they remember the time they were worshiped as gods.

This is a Mau cat. It is a member of an ancient breed that lived in Ancient Egypt.

Cat goddess

More than 300,000 mummified cats were discovered in a ruined temple in northern Egypt.

Thousands of years ago, the Ancient Egyptians worshiped the cat goddess Bastet. She was the daughter of Ra, the Sun god, and she protected him each night as he made his way through the underworld to rise again the next day. The Egyptians said that Bastet kept the Sun's flame alive at night in her eyes.

Black magic

The cat's piercing gaze provoked fear and hostility in the Middle Ages. In 1233, Pope Gregory IX decreed that black cats were the Devil's workers, and many people believed they were witches in disguise. Across Europe, cats were caught and burned alive.

So many cats were killed in the Middle Ages that disease-spreading rats swarmed the towns.

This sped the spread of the Black Death, a terrible plague that killed about half the people in Europe in the 14th century. The disease was carried on flea-infested rats, which were running rampant because there were fewer cats around to kill them.

In Japan, Beckoning Cat figurines are said to bring good luck to their owners.

Fortune cats

The Beckoning Cat, or "maneki neko," is a sculpture of the Japanese goddess of mercy. Legend tells that one day a certain lord was walking down the street, when he passed a cat sitting in a temple doorway. The cat beckoned him over, and as he moved, a bolt of lightning ripped through the sky and struck the spot where he'd been standing.

A group of kittens is sometimes called a "kindle," while a group of cats is a "clowder."

Feline facts

Here are some intriguing and extraordinary facts that you may not know about cats.

Weighty issues

Singapuras are the lightest breed of cat. At around 3kg (6lb), a fully-grown Singapura weighs about the same as a six-month-old kitten of an average-sized breed.

Maine Coons are the world's heaviest domesticated cats. Males can reach a weight of 12kg (26lb) and their bodies can grow over 1m (3ft) long, which is about as big as a lynx.

These little Maine Coon kittens will grow huge, but will take four or five years to reach full size.

Ear-twisting

Of the 517 muscles in a cat's body, 60 of those are in its ears. A cat can turn its ears 180 degrees, positioning them to face any sound it detects.

Most cats have an amazing ability to find their way back home even after traveling long distances over unfamiliar territory. No one really knows how they do this.

Mouth organs

As well as smelling with its nose, a cat also smells with a part of its mouth, called a Jacobson's organ. This is why you might see your cat curl up its mouth and "sneer" when it senses a strong odor.

A sleepy life

Cats spend around 50% of their lives dozing, 15% in deep sleep, and 30% grooming themselves. That means they spend just 5% of their time on the rest of their activities, such as eating and playing.

Around 65% of a cat's life is spent snoozing.

Big families

An American tabby named Dusty, from Texas, had the largest ever cat family, giving birth to around 420 kittens during her lifetime. She had her last litter at the grand old age of 18, which is about 85 in human terms.

In its lifetime, an average female cat can have more than 100 kittens.

63

INDEX

ACKNOWLEDGEMENTS

Additional writing by Simon Tudhope

American editorial by Carrie Armstrong

Cover design by Joanne Kirkby

With thanks to Charlotte Thomas

PHOTO CREDITS